# We Live With Nana And Grandpa

Written by Beth Jester

Illustrated by Rylan Fabryk

ISBN 978-1-63814-988-0 (Paperback)
ISBN 978-1-63814-990-3 (Hardcover)
ISBN 978-1-63814-989-7 (Digital)

Covenant Books
11661 Hwy 707
Murrells Inlet, SC 29576
www.covenantbooks.com

My name is Sophia, and I am five years old. My brother, Aiden, is three, and we live with our nana and grandpa.

We have a swing set in our yard.

Our dog's name is Layla. Our cat is Maxine.

At the end of the day, my friends at school have a daddy or a mommy pick them up.

Nana always picks my brother and me up from school.
Sometimes, Grandpa picks us up.

Grandpa says some kids' families look
different from other kids' families.

We like to ride our bikes around the block or in the driveway after school.

My bike is orange. Aiden's is blue.

I like unicorns, and Aiden likes fire trucks.

My favorite dinner is pizza. Mmmm.

I have my own bed and bedroom.

Aiden does too.

Nana's friend is Grammy. Her grandson, Jackson, lives with her.

His grampy and Jackson's dad live with them too.

Jackson is our friend. We are going to his birthday party on Saturday. It's at a bouncy house. He will be five like me.

Mrs. B. at the food store has hair like Nana's. She is nice. She says her granddaughter, Emma, who is two years old, lives with her. Mrs. B. and Nana talk when we go to the store.

I want Mommy to live with us.

Sometimes I cry at night
because I miss my mommy.

I am sad or mad or wake up with scary dreams some mornings, but Nana or Grandpa hug me and it makes me feel better.

Grandpa says that he and Nana will always be here for us.

They say, "We love you both, always and forever."

At bedtime, Nana gives us a bath and washes our hair.

After we are clean, we say our prayers, read a book, and we each get to pick a subject for Nana to tell us a story.

Nana says, "Good night and God bless you." Grandpa and Nana both give us hugs and kisses, and we roll over to sleep.

I want to thank God for His nudging me to write this book!

My hope is that the words on these pages have helped children understand that families can look different. Children in some families are raised by their grandparents or others. As of this spring, 2022 my husband, John and I will have been raising these two on the left for almost seven years. This is a picture of me, the Author of this children's book, Beth Jester with Kianna and Kayden, two of our grandchildren who inspired me to write this book. In addition, they also inspired me to start the Support Group below.

I'd like to thank all those who have encouraged me with their expertise, experience, willingness and support to complete this writing and publishing journey: John Jester, Joclyn Jester, Marie Mueller, Laurie Pepe, Jamie Bendas and my parents Alan Cherry (Children's Author) and Beth Cherry.

These are all my grandchildren on Christmas, 2021. Clockwise: Baby Noah, Harrison, Lillian, JP, Kayden, Ryan and Kianna.

BC Grand Families Support Group www.Facebook.com/BCGrandfamilies located in Bucks County, Pennsylvania. Feel free to contact me at BCGrandfamilies@gmail.com. I'm happy to share resources and support with others.

Please have your child(ren) draw us a picture of what their family looks like...

Make sure to tag us on Instagram @BCGrandfamilies so we can feature your picture!

Printed in the USA
CPSIA information can be obtained
at www.ICGtesting.com
LVHW070221131023
760650LV00024B/36